BOOSEY & HAWKES
CHORAL TREASURY

Howells: *A New Year carol*
two-part chorus & piano

UPPER VOICES

FFICULTY: ★★☆☆☆

Herbert Howells
A New Year carol

for two-part chorus & piano

I0809644

BOOSEY & HAWKES

Published by Boosey & Hawkes Music Publishers Ltd
Aldwych House
71–91 Aldwych
London
WC2B 4HN

www.boosey.com

AN IMAGEM COMPANY

ISMN 979-0-060-12353-5
ISBN 978-0-85162-810-3

This impression 2013

Printed in England by The Halstan Printing Group, Amersham, Bucks

Notesetting by The Note Factory

Text

Here we bring new water from the well so clear
For to worship God with, this happy New Year.
Sing levvy dew, sing levvy dew, the water and the wine;
The seven bright gold wires and the bugles that do shine.

Sing reign of Fair Maid with gold upon her toe,
Open you the West Door and turn the Old Year go.

Sing reign of Fair Maid with gold upon her chin,
Open you the East Door and let the New Year in.
Sing levvy dew...

Traditional

A NEW YEAR CAROL

Two-part song

Traditional words

Music by
HERBERT HOWELLS

9
mf
worship God with, this happy New Year. Sing levy dew, sing
mf
worship God with, this happy New Year. Sing levy dew, sing
14
cresc
levy dew, the water and the wine; The seven bright gold
cresc
levy dew, the water and the wine; The seven bright gold
cresc
18
f
wires and the bugles that do shine. Sing reign of
f
wires and the bugles that do shine. Sing reign of Fair Maid with

Fair Maid, O - pen you the West Door
gold up-on her toe, O - pen you the West Door
and turn the Old Year go.
and turn the Old Year go.
ff
mp
f

36
mp
Sing reign of Fair Maid with gold up-on her
Sing reign of Fair Maid with gold up-on her
mp
sim
40
mf
chin, O-pen you the East Door and let the New Year
chin, O-pen you the East Door and let the New Year
mf
44
mf cresc
in. Sing lev - y dew, sing lev - y dew, the wa - ter and the
in. Sing lev - y dew, sing lev - y dew, the wa - ter and the
p cresc

48
wine; The _ sev-en bright gold wires and the bu - gles that do
wine; The _ sev-en bright gold wires and the bu - gles that do
52
shine. ___ Sing reign ___ of Fair ___
shine. ___ Sing _ reign of Fair Maid with gold up-on her
56
Maid, ___ O - pen the West _ Door ___ and
toe, ___ O - pen thou the West _ Door ___ and
2/4
3/4

turn the Old Year go. Sing of
turn the Old Year go. Sing of
allarg
Fair Maid, O - pen you the West Door and
Fair Maid, O - pen you the West Door and
allarg
(allarg) a tempo
let the New Year in.
let the New Year in.
(allarg) a tempo

BOOSEY & HAWKES CHORAL TREASURY

Drawing upon a rich archive, the *Boosey & Hawkes Choral Treasury* presents a wealth of exciting choral opportunities for choirs of all types and abilities wishing to explore new choral territories. A perfect resource for accessible and inspiring choral masterworks of the twentieth century and beyond, this series restores many difficult to obtain sacred and secular classics to the repertoire.

Choral music by Herbert Howells in the Boosey & Hawkes Choral Treasury

Good counsel	unison voices & piano	979-0-060-12351-1
Irish wren song	two-part chorus & piano	979-0-060-12352-8
A New Year carol	two-part chorus & piano	979-0-060-12353-5
Piping down the valleys wild	two-part chorus & piano	979-0-060-12354-2
Creep afore ye gang	SAATTBB a cappella	979-0-060-12350-4
The Shadows	SSAATTBB a cappella	979-0-060-12360-3

Selected choral music for upper voices from Boosey & Hawkes

Stephen Adams	*The Holy City* (SA/SSA & piano)	979-0-060-01005-7/01008-8
Gwyn Arch	*Four Negro Spirituals* (SSA & piano)	979-0-060-01039-2
Bela Bartok	*Enchanting song* (SSA a cappella)	979-0-060-01153-5
	Spring (SSA a cappella)	979-0-060-01227-3
	The Wooing of a girl (SSA a cappella)	979-0-060-01256-3
May Brahe	*Bless this house* (SA & piano)	979-0-051-41449-9
Benjamin Britten	*Friday Afternoons* (1–4 parts & piano)	979-0-060-10500-5
	A Ceremony of Carols (SSA & harp/piano)	979-0-060-01410-9
	O can ye sew cushions? (SSA & piano)	979-0-051-45213-2
Aaron Copland	*Old American Songs* suite I (SA & piano)	979-0-051-47699-2
	Old American Songs suite II (SA & piano)	979-0-051-47803-3
Gerald Finzi	*Let us now praise famous men* (SA & piano)	979-0-060-03035-2
	Ten children's songs (SS & piano)	979-0-060-11036-8
Michael Head	*The little road to Bethlehem* (SA & piano)	979-0-060-03241-7
	The ships of Arcady (SSA & piano)	979-0-060-03263-9
	Star Candles (SA & piano)	979-0-060-03268-4
John Ireland	*Ex ore innocentium* (SS & piano)	979-0-060-03371-1
Zoltán Kodály	*Evening song* (SSA a cappella)	979-0-060-03515-9
	Hippity-hoppity (SSA a cappella)	979-0-060-03529-6
	Mountain nights (SSSSA a cappella)	979-0-060-03577-7
Bohuslav Martinu	*Three sacred songs* (SSA & violin)	979-0-060-03697-2
Peter Maxwell Davies	*Five carols* (SSA a cappella)	979-0-060-03749-8
Elizabeth Poston	*Dance to your daddie* (SA & piano)	979-0-060-02032-2
Roger Quilter	*Non nobis Domine* (unison/SSA & piano)	979-0-060-02180-0/02179-4
Ralph Vaughan Williams	*Linden Lea* (unis/SS/SSA & piano)	979-0-060-08972-5/02849-6/02848-9

BH 12353

ISBN 978-0-85162-810-3

9 780851 628103

BOOSEY & HAWKES

AN IMAGEM COMPANY

DISTRIBUTED BY HAL LEONARD

8 84088 99585 0

48022699 M060123535